At the Side of the Road

Michael Anthony Adams, Jr.

SIX SEEDS PRESS
Baltimore, MD

First Six Seeds Press Edition
Copyright © 1999 Michael Anthony Adams, Jr.

Originally Published as *Andrew's Songs, Vol I.: At the Side of the Road* by Michael Anthony Adams, Jr. by CreateSpace Independent Publishing Platform
December 2011

Previously Published under the Pen Name Israfel Sivad by CreateSpace Independent Publishing Platform
April 2012

Current Edition Published by Six Seeds Press,
Baltimore, MD
February 2022

All rights reserved.

ISBN: 978-1-952240-03-4

Cover Design © 2022 PJ Adams
Portrait of Michael Anthony Adams, Jr. © 2014 PJ Adams

Also by Michael Anthony Adams, Jr. and Published by Six Seeds Press

Fiction:
The Adversary's Good News: A Novel
Psychedelicizations: Short Stories
The American Apocalypse: Short Stories
Crossroads Blues: A Novel
The Cars Behind, Beside Us: Short Stories
Welcome to the Modern World, Charlie: Short Stories
Notes from the Idle Mind: Short Stories

Nonfiction:
Disorder: An Avant-Garde Memoir of Psychosis, Healing and Love

Poetry:
We Are the Underground: Poems
From Now to You: Haiku
Recipe for a Future Theogony: Poems
Indigo Glow: Poems
The Tree Outside My Window: Poems
At the Side of the Road: Poems
Soundtrack for the New Millennium: A Poem

www.6SeedsPress.com

At the Side of the Road
For You

Alone	9
The Joke	10
The Side of the Road	12
A Cloudy Evening	14
The Pauper Prince	15
More than Once	16
A Child's Poem	18
Black Carpet	19
Stretch	20
A Distinction	22
Highway Poem	24
Black	25
The Construction	26
Nursery Rhyme	28
Natural Art	29
Brothers	30
The Vulnerable, White Underside	31
The Poets	32
Carpe Diem	33
Lisa	35
All I Ever See	37
Melodious Music of Beauty	39
Murder	40
Summer's Day	41
A Moment's Second	42
Light Seeps In	43
The Couple Passing By	44
Far from Me	45
A Lesson Taught	46
Tormenting Time	47
To Another	48

Dreaming Illusions	49
Break Through	50
Love Letter	51
Something Small	52
Imprisoned	53
The Student's Lesson	54

At the Side of the Road

Alone

Sitting alone. Always to think –
I always have and always will.
Thinking of places life's been through,
thinking of people I once knew,
and then, my thoughts will turn to You…

The Joke

Suddenly –
as suddenly as a silent cat springs
upon a feeble mouse who is innocently
clutching a seed in hands meaning no harm –
I heard a knock upon my door.

With the sounds of music pulsing into my ears,
swirling into my head, and reaching every inch of my body,
I approached the door separating myself
from the rest of the world –
So innocent… I never suspected this world to bring pain.
So naively I assumed, the way only a child assumes,
that I heard a faint laughter waiting to
suck me into its joke on the other side.
So, inside the safety of my room, I
gave a slight chuckle opening the door
between myself and the joke.

How strange it is to think
that as a ten year old I mistook
the heavy sobs of my mother's tears
for a joke that she wanted me to be a part of.
However, as the door finished its creak upon
the hinges, I saw her face distorted:
eyes swelled from a flood of tears
produced by torrential rains,
her face so twisted that
it appeared her soul was being
stretched upon a medieval torturer's rack.
And what I mistook for her jovial laugh
were the sobs of a woman who could not understand
why God would do *this* to *her*.

She said to me, "Grandma's on the phone for you."
Like a robot, I walked into the kitchen
and held the yellow receiver against my ear –
"Hello," I spoke into the machine.
My grandmother greeted me with the news
I knew would crackle into my ear from
somewhere far away. I set the phone down.
I remember my mom returned shortly thereafter,
no longer making the sounds that I mistook for laughter,
and told my grandmother I was in shock.
But I just stared out the window at our
deck shining brightly in the sun,
at the fence that kept me from ever really knowing my neighbors,
and couldn't believe my grandfather was dead.

The Side of the Road

And silently, while sitting as I read a book,
I gazed upon the sunlight
breaking through the trees and casting its glow upon
the concrete where I sat
while the tarry, blackened road seemed to melt into
a sticky mass by my feet.
And I remained so content, sitting there, reading
at the side of the road.

Reading a book at the side of the road,
waiting for reason, nothing makes me move
unless something strikes to make me move.
There came no reason to, but one not to.

All these metal monsters,
they knew where they had to go.
At least, it seemed they did.
They hurried to get there:
a screech around the turn,
a burst of wind as they passed me,
a scream as they flew away from the stop sign halting their
　　progress.
How could they be so sure of where they had to go that
　　they could move so fast?

And that's where the answer occurred to me –
not in the words of the book I read,
not in the birds who chirped their own answers.
I discovered why not to move
as I viewed those metal monsters.
They didn't know where they were going.
They didn't care where they were going.
They just knew they had to arrive there soon.

And I decided that I'd rather read my book.

A Cloudy Evening

See, all I think I want is just your love.
All my eyes can see is not seen clearly,
and I'm so scared that what I see is never love.

If I could think the truth, then I could rest.
No thing that I can think eases my thinking.
So surety says surety just isn't sure.

And now my love and life hold me common.
Love confuses some while life confuses more.
One pierces my side; one comforts my weary head.

If you know something, tell me now
because which does which I just don't know.
Which is right, I think I'll never know.

The Pauper Prince

Love is a beggar, ruling like a prince,
living, misleading with this role at which it plays:
a monarch that must sleep in gutters since
its lie never ceases through varied days.
And it will never state its subject soul,
asking subjects to give their lives to prove
that begging is what gives it control –
We live and breathe and die for missing love.

…And love lives too much to fit into this harsh strictness.
It doesn't love itself.
A self that's never known
since to poor beggars
desire's never shown.
Maybe a confused, pauper prince never truly exists…

But pain and hurt and hope prove charity,
and need and greed and loss live jealously,
and want and lust and art and poetry
would tell their sordid tales differently.
    I search my heart to find that love once stole
    and now it can control its own, my soul.

More Than Once

Lost. A seed by chance was stolen,
blown by wind streams softly gusting,
landing lonely, to awake in
barren fields where silent dust sings.
Here, amidst a dearth of dreary,
here, the earth, for rain, begs, lusting,
here, where skies whisper with weary,
life lives only death dying slowly.
Far from home, that seed wind buried.
Desolation strains to scarcely
breed a parasitic thirsting
breathing what lives stolen only,
leaving thieves forever starving.
Now these torments plague another
helpless sapling feeling living
wrenched away… This lifeless reservoir's
weeds slowly strangle, bit by bit
by means of choking scavengers.
Roots reach forth in pain's gasping fits.
Struggling towards heaven's open land,
I choked and died.

(When I looked away to search the darkness,
I stumbled in the gravel on my downward slope.
I landed face first in sharpened mud
to scream against my own false step,
to bleed amid earthen rocks,
and you stood above me…
Like the sun to trees reaching towards it,
a beam of light caught hold of my hand.)

More than once, I've lost my way down different
paths of life by slipping in rock-strewn sands,

falling to live on this lifeless descent
where starving stones supply a barren field.
And more than once, I was scared, lonely, sent
to grow alone with weeds whose roots will steal
my life, now young, though stumbled, still begun –
A piece in pieces that may never heal.
But more than once, always, you've stood right there
to ease this starving soul who gasps for air.

A Child's Poem

Stretch and bend
for the light of the sun.
Your hands reach up
searching the heavens.
You gave your care to what you loved,
and sometimes what you loved was me.

Your arms cradle what you cherish.
Sing to the ear sweet melodies.
And now I miss your time's resting
embrace through painful memories.

Whispers clued us to your thoughts,
but no one listened.
I tried to hear those words.
I heard a shy swish.
You spoke
only love.

It proved the peace inside of you
to move through all the world I see.
It made me wish what you possess
could someday live inside of me.

Black Carpet

Roll out the black carpet.
Begin the elegant times:

Sucking smoke through parched lips.
A needle thrust through sweating skin.
For once in a dream – Feel…

Through the clouds where falling, feeling, grabbing hold
finds nothing solid in the silk to grab.
Through the skies where reaching must something grab
    hold,
but there's nothing in emptiness to grab.

This beating, breaking heart…
These softly stolen sighs…
A life fallen apart…

Nothing left to say, and nothing more to do.
Land broken by the final force's hit.
Land broken by the pageantry's dark show
by landing broken on reality below.

Around a body soul
roll up the black carpet.
End the elegant times.

Stretch

The winds will blow their weight around outside,
but true storms build somewhere inside the clouds.
The rain we see is only the excess –
And now it's pouring down outside my room.

"I'm not looking for your sympathy. I just want you to
    listen."

I listened. I didn't know what to do.
All I know is what I know; so little
except that life is always spent in pain…
And love, and strength, and fear, and happiness,
and sorrow, and sometimes there's misery.
Life simply is. The truth is: so is death.
I couldn't tell *him* that. I wouldn't dare.
All he wanted was for me to listen.

"All these people keep staring at me,
but they don't wanna fight…
They don't wanna knock me down when I yell."

You know what? You want to know a secret?
I'll whisper: *Stretch is going to kill himself.*

"I'm sick of drugs, alcohol, fornication,
bisexuality, prison, pain, life.
I don't want this life."

The rain pours down outside my room.
The darkness hints sometimes it's moving past.
It lets the sun break light between the clouds,
but today's windy day is overcast.
The rain is falling, dripping through gutters,
washing through the drain outside my window.

The sun, surely, will live again someday
for me, for now, that's true I somehow know.

"See, this is my reality, man."

But clouds darken the stormy skies,
and the wind is blowing hard once again.
It's God I thank for what He's given me…
But now, it looks like there will be more rain.

A Distinction

Here's distinction between my love and hate:
Somewhere beyond right here there lives a tree,
and yet, between our bodies stands a fence.
Atop the links, signs warn (NO TRESPASSING).
I'll use my feet to climb that barrier,
to leave behind the strictness of this world.

Standing amid ringing petals of tiny sun drops,
(man's harsh life reminding my mind;
it's pushing forward from behind).
I'm lost to nature:
hearing wild birds chirping,
feeling wistful winds swirling,
seeing clouds living high in cotton luster…
A lonely bush beside a broken, fallen tree –
sensing serenity that flows from them to me.

It flows in trickles of a stream
that drips and drops waters at dark distances.
And to that singing source I'm drawn
through scorns of brambles slicing my ankles,
leaving blood to wash my feet…
Why would the woods do that to me?
And did you know that it's because
what I thought was a creek is a sewer
– what I thought was behind is before –
the thorns recognized my steps:
an intruder, their enemy, the human.

Realizing, knowing that I despise
everything my species is standing for,
I want to hide in this sanctuary
of dreaming trees until there's room to be

among our pompous, lost society…
If only these woods would still consume me.

Highway Poem

It's hard to reach you when this highway shakes my hand,
and it's hard to see when this world flies past so fast,
and it's hard to talk above the wind ruffling your hair,
and it's hard to care when everything will always change.

Sometimes I want this trip to stop –
just settle down and let me breathe my life
because I think I saw a flower blurred outside,
and I want to steal some time to steal a look at it.

I need to stop this trip to step outside and smell a scent –
I need to stop this car to stretch my legs and see the
    sights –
I need to stop my mind to let it simply sit –
because I need to stop my life and take a look at that flower
    again.

Black

Staring at the blackness of night,
are you thinking of the loneliness passed?

Do you remember yesterday
in the subtle black of a big city:
the wild nights of LA or the lighted black of Vegas?

Perhaps, you remember our black,
our black in the nights of horror…
movies or reality for the black was both.

But do you remember long ago?
The lonely nights of pure black:
black leather, black tee shirts, and black hearts…

And what of tomorrow?
The black of our wetsuits on the surfboards
in the black of night, the jet black water and the cool air.

Do you remember these things
as you're staring at the blackness of night?

The Construction

First, let's lay a strong foundation.
Nothing can be supported by something of lesser
 strength…
both would crumble from existence.

Now, let's build the walls high,
build them sturdy, build them strong, again nothing is weak.
That way, with strength, it will stand.

We must place a roof on top,
one that's solid and hard so that nothing can get through;
we can't have the world crash down on us.

Now, we can cut the windows.
We want to be protected, but we want to see everything we
 can.
Because we might see something we like…

That's why we have doors.
That way, when we like what we see, we can leave and get
 it.
Who doesn't want to ever leave their home?

Heat, electricity, water – of course!
We need all the modern conveniences; life's just to be
 enjoyed.
But sometimes, things don't stay…

That's where insulation comes in.
All of us need to be warm, happy, content – insulate! Stay
 warm.
Of course, that's obvious.

Paint the outside pretty.

That's what everybody sees. That's what really counts.
There's more to the outside though.

We also have to landscape
because, at the very least, we all want to *seem* attractive.
But you already knew that!

Of course, though, even with
the strength, the heat, the beauty, it can all be destroyed…
with one sweep of the wrecking ball.

Nursery Rhyme

A life like Humpty Dumpty...
simply straddling a wall,
but I fell to break my crown –
no longer king of all.
And although the people tried,
they couldn't put me back together again.

Lost way down at the bottom;
I was so weak from my thirst.
I turned to climb that hill,
but before we reached the well,
I stumbled within sight of the fountain.
Down, down to the very bottom I fell.

My pockets too full of posy...
that's what it was. For with
ashes and ashes, we all
fall down. From me I took that
which kept me down, and I climbed
to the top to live my Humpty Dumpty life again.

Natural Art

Hostile waves form and fall, passing underneath
the dolphins, dear friends, perform their circus
while I'm waiting for my soul to fly free.

The wave comes in from the edge of sight.
I paddle to get caught in its surge.
From off the back of the swell I begin
to fall. My legs fly upright, and I'm propelled

down the face. Speed like never before… A
dream? No, in a dream, I would not feel the
wind. To the bottom where I fly back to
the face. Carving, floating, the speed… And death.

Paddling back to my only place of peace,
I perform once again my natural art.

Brothers

The boys sit on the wall
with smiles tickling their lips.
Between them sits the beautiful, black dog –
alert to protect the ones he loves:
the two brothers in the coonskin caps.

Forever, now, in this photograph
live two boys seated on a wall
with smiles tickling their lips.

And between them will always sit
this beautiful, black dog…
alert here even when his body grows old,
ready to protect those he loves
and those who love him.

The Vulnerable, White Underside

Her ancient strength bred from years of turmoil…
her thin, long muscles stretching taut with every step,
ending in the shining, pointed nails made to rip my flesh –
the vulnerable, white underside.

Her eyes pierce me to the quick:
green rimmed black with the glow of the wild.
As she watches me, I fear she sees my soul –
the vulnerable, white underside.

The Poets

I exercise my right not to walk,
and therefore exercise my right not to conform.

We are the actor, the rebel, the lover,
the red-headed kid with glasses,
the tall, brown-haired kid with a buzz cut.
We are the shy, new kid at school.
But most important of all,
we are the romantic poets who cannot conform.

Our poetry comes from within our souls;
it manifests itself in a barrage of emotions
that no one can control.
We each add our separate verse
as we free-write our lives
so that we may live for today,
so that we may seize the day.

Carpe Diem

What should I do? What could I do?
What can anyone ever do
other than to love and to live?

We must love pitter-patter rain
as it beats upon rich, green leaves
of towering forests of trees
that filter the sun into dots
of light upon the earthen soil
beneath our stomping stepping feet.

We must love the powerful form
of the cat as it slinks through our
backyards on its soft and lithe paws
with its shining coat drawing the
sun into each follicle to
reflect its own darkened light back.

We must love the beautiful form
of humans with our radiant
skins covering sublime muscles
that protect our fragile souls from
the pain that surrounds every
physical action – thought movement.

We must live life! We must shout loud!
From eternal depths of our souls,
we must shout out that we are free.
We must be free that we may live.
We shed our clothes, hair, and our skins,
our bones, and all else but our souls.

For in our souls, there we are free.
There, hidden deep inside ourselves

we are all the same, with the same
fears, loves, joys, insecurities,
and with the same need to live life.
Yes, we must live, and we must love.

We must not leave a stone unturned;
we must not leave a thought unthought.
Leaving no action untaken,
never, not ever, never must
we turn from the paths that we have
chosen for ourselves… For Ourselves!

Lisa

She was my conscience
floating past my body
in that smoke-filled prison of a room.
There was a moment – was it less than a second?
There was a moment when I could have sworn
she was really you.

(Across the table from where I confessed,
crying with the remembrance of my sin,
I needed you, my conscience, to forgive
me because I could not forgive again.)

Did she remember? One night in a dark room,
bending down to grab her shoes, using her hand
to push her curls off her face,
I told her she reminded me of you.
I said that, from the back, you both looked the same,
that, for a moment, when she spoke,
she spoke to me with words that you always used.

(If love could prove its truth with salvation,
then my soul would have been saved by your face.
If love could pronounce a judgment,
then my soul would have been judged by your gaze.)

In the confines of acquaintances,
stumbling through bodies and faces,
tumbling into a haze of which
I wanted to become a part –
any part, if it was a part that could hide.
A body or a bottle, please just let me hide.
Don't let me see myself…

(But, for a moment, her face became yours,

and when you turned her head so not to see,
I realized that you would never judge.
Always, it was me judging me.)

All I Ever See

A sunrise crosses across the ocean,
casts golden mirrors of reflections in
endless waves stretching till they have no end.
Building white force, rushing up towards the shore,
they rear their heads to crash such a display:
the sea's voice screams at waiting, silent sands.
You know, I waited up all the past night,
needing a glimpse, a peak at true beauty,
and now that day has finally arrived,
my soul is left feeling unsatisfied.

A small clearing lives inside this forest;
one where light sheds shadows of dancing leaves.
There's peace, protection as my body sits,
reclining, resting on these fallen trees.
Missing the branches crackling underfoot
as I walked here, silent, I contemplate.
Staring at such nature as surrounds me,
I realize all this hides beauty's face.
It's the world itself that distracts my mind.
Bodies keep me from what my heart can find.

And then, upon a summer, Southern night,
while I sat there amid the thickening dew,
looking across the darkening of the world
(the violining crickets start anew –
so tired, their tugging tunes upon my soul),
I felt myself beginning to lose my grasp
upon this slowly fading illusion.
My mind fought on harder, trying to clasp
this world that I, yet barely, blearily,
continued contemplating dreamily.

And there, inside a corner of my mind,
beneath shores of reality, a place
only my heart could ever hope to find,
I saw a dreaming halo round your face.
My mind had searched for years to see this sight,
to see beauty so bright it is the sun.
But I have always turned from blinding light
to see the night. In darkness, you won.
Somehow, somewhere, you pulled my soul from me
to see what I could never see before.
What is the truest beauty man can see?
It's only that blinding forever more.
 And you are all that I will ever see
 for it is your beauty that blinded me.

Melodious Music of Beauty

The fingers stretch forth from the veins of knuckles at the end of the rivers of veins.
They fly across the white and black to make the melodious music of beauty.
This clearing in the hostile jungle is the only peace in this violent world of pain.
A question stutters through my pursed lips, "Wh-what are you doing with that beast in here?"
The only response I never imagined meets me: "Why, I make the melodious music of beauty you hear."

Murder

I slide into the flesh, and out slips the
moan. Through the skin I slice. The scream pierces
my soul. I bury my weapon to the
base, and my excitement gets excited.
So I pull the form out and thrust it back...
deeper! A scream... twice the first! Out I come
again, and the life fluid seeps. I plunge
back... AGAIN! AGAIN! AGAIN! AGAIN! And...
I thrust in and out, slice back and forth! The
screams are in a frenzy. Finally, with
fluid covering us both... it all stops.
...
    (Until, once more, I feel the urge for sin...
    until, once more, I feel that urge again.)

Summer's Day

I tried to write a sonnet for you.
I wanted it complete in every word.
I wanted this to be perfect for you,
but time ran off in unsaid words.
Maybe, if I had more time to sit here,
the words finishing these lines
would make this poem complete and clear,
but for now, this is all I know to say:

Sometimes, it's best to keep things short.
Sometimes, it's best not to have an end.
Sometimes, the words will say too much,
and then they mean nothing.
    Maybe we could complete this poem someday,
    someday, when there's time for a summer's day…

A Moment's Second

A moment's second could be all of time
if it were time I spent inside your arms,
but time ceases among the realms where rhyme
cannot attempt to conjure up the charms.
So, there, resting asleep in nameless space,
I'm lost amid peaceful eternity.
It's when we leave that I must turn to face
this time that pushes on reality.

Is that what we both wish to soon escape?
It's that from which I tried to run away,
hiding between your arms' embraces' scape.
But now I have returned to face the day:
    always the same, always so full of pain,
    the reason that I'll run to you again.

Light Seeps In

It was a glimpse of you that stole my mind
away from me amid this toilsome dream,
and soon I lay awake with hopes to find
the source that sprung this swell through my thought
    stream.
So slowly, very slowly, light seeps in –
My eyes opened to see I lay alone.
Was it a dream? A dream to have again
if, somehow, by dreams reality's grown.

Now, tell me how I thought those things that night.
(How quickly fantasies will lose their shape.)
That night, I needed you within my sight
while now I have no need of your escape.
    Can you forgive me for mistaken thoughts?
    Or is it true that thought's mistaken not?

The Couple Passing By

He pulls her closer as they walk on by.
His tensing hand somehow sensing my eyes,
but I look anyways. Forcing her close,
it seems he feels he must protect his prize.
Yet she simply brings her head more erect,
walking more stately as she's passing by.
Chest thrust forward, hips now swivel
beneath the fabric under which they lie.
Her neck turns a passing glance towards me,
her irises begging to realize
that (while her body gives a full, healthy banquet)
this feast is meant only for my two eyes.
    She'll never let me sense her with my hand.
    Sadly, that's what he'll never understand.

Far from Me

A will to live a love
is all I wish to do.
That love returned to me
is all I ask of you,

but love will never stay;
it moves and flows and leaves –
running here, then to there,
then running far from me…

A Lesson Taught

One to two, from two to three…
It always came back to you.

All these things inside of me,
they never escaped from you.

Love once thought – a lesson taught –
that always returned to you.

Tormenting Time

To torment time, I tempt myself with morbid dreams
of moves I made in bed, and now it seems I'll
tempt my head back to this narrow bed:

Lustily, I lost myself to a loose lipped girl
whose lips loved like a glove. I stretched her sieve of silken
flesh across my soul, and I slipped right through that
    hole…

To Another

An emotion is like faith:
you either have it or you don't.

And if you can't see it,
that doesn't make it less real.

You can't explain why you have a feeling,
but if you do, you can't deny its fact,

and you can never communicate
your faith, your heart to another.

Dreaming Illusions

Wake my head at rest:
stolen mind, bleeding paper:
dreaming illusions.

Break Through

Pull me, twist me, blind me, bind me…
spread cross the abyss and heaving,
teetering above this crevasse
just to make a piece of art breathe:

Words come too hard to mean nothing.
When spoken, they fall on deaf ears,
and when I sense your senses, dear,
you listen but refuse to hear.

These words are all I'll ever have
to hold forth pieces of my soul.
They stretch, reach tired arms to you,
to your heart where they can't break through.

Love Letter

A poem for letters of life
that pierce your heart to bleed your soul
with words that say as much as life –
saying nothing, nothing at all.

But if waiting takes long enough,
if, somehow, tomorrow will come
with time to read these words again,
then, maybe, they'll mean something more.

Something Small

From the back she looks like her…
It's always from the back.

If I had never seen your face,
who knows how this page would read.
But now I see you in everybody's back.

I'd like to take a piece of something small
and make it so much larger than it is.
But that's not the way I think.
It's not the way I am.

So I sit here and look at scraggles
of your hair hanging loose
in the way you always pull it back…
And I try to see what it all means,
to take this scene and make it mean
so much more than it really does.

But here's the truth…
This scene means to me
what you do now…

Nothing
other than a back without a face,
something that I'll never scrutinize again.

Imprisoned

Imprisoned by a thought I never thought,
and beauty lost itself inside my mind.
Time trickles tears to try to wipe away
this life that stole the light to leave me blind
to everything living both in and out.
An unknown sun – nothing reflects its rays.
In darkness, with a fool's soul that found
a cell and dwells where freedom's bounty stays.

Freedom chained me to myself.
Ignorance: The jailer of liberty.
Darkness still, begging to see, tears spill
from eyes that cry for things
taken before they were shown.
Captive to enthrallment,
captured by misleading truth –
I reached forward trying to grasp
at something new,
sacrificed beauty for freedom,
but beauty I never knew.
Now, I must know if beauty's found in truth.

For, once, so long ago it seems, naïve
in thought, believing freedom's dream, I fell
where darkened depths clank fetters round the soul…
Within a cell, I woke to find this hell.
Thus bound and blind by thoughts that know nothing,
my mind attempts to find reality.
Although my hands write ruled, my pen holds fast
to find a form for truth that frees its beauty.

The Student's Lesson

A teacher addressed his student,
his tone as sharp as a razor,
"Raise your eyes to mine, young man,
and examine Cupid's quiver!
Speak out on romance, on feelings –
all things that you know nothing of…
But speak! It's obvious to us,
you can't possibly speak on love!"

The student grew red in his face
contemplating his thoughts' sources:
abandonment, worldly love.
He cleared his throat, feeling a mouse
for he had never been *in* love –
began to begin his sermon,
but first, prayed to his only friend:
God, please let me teach this lesson.

He began, "Teacher so very wise,
so very learned, a scholar,
ask me to speak to you of love,
which to show me no one bothered…
not you, parents, peers, nor myself.
Only God reveals his lessons;
for love only He has shown me."
Here began the student's lesson.

"So I know nothing of your love,"
such words shaking the student's voice,
"For only have I felt our pain,
but if I could have had a choice
I would surrender my knowledge,
retaining my will to press on,

for love to be shown me just once.
Thus, the first step of God's lesson.

"An imitation I could make –
to imitate is not to feel.
Remember, this is what I say:
Love can't be false… only real.
So I know nothing of your love.
But pain makes my mind a prison.
Love slips through the lock on pain's door
to open the student's lesson.

"I'll never be as read as yourself,
be the Don Juan some call themselves.
Mother, father may feel nothing,
may feel nothing for this self.
So you can laugh. Yes, you can jest,
can make me a mat to step on…
But God's behind the prison door.
That, friends, is the student's lesson."

The teacher sat still and pondered,
thinking of his life dropped a tear.
In a voice so shaky and weak
that the students could barely hear,
he spoke so true, for once, so sweet
to tell his student his lesson,
"My son, I am the student, too:
the heart of the student's lesson."

Portrait by PJ Adams

About the Author

Michael Anthony Adams, Jr. is originally from Whittier, CA. He holds a master's degree in Philosophy from the New School for Social Research in New York City. As a teenager, he was the lead vocalist and lyricist for Richmond, VA-based hardcore band Broken Chains of Segregation. In 2012, he began publishing his collected works under the pen name Israfel Sivad. He's the founder of Ursprung Collective, a spoken word/music project referred to as "fantastic brain food" on ReverbNation. He was the primary lyricist on indie rock group One & the Many's first two albums, *Forms* and *Hours*. His writing has appeared in the *Santa Fe Literary Review*, *The Stray Branch*, *Badlands Literary Journal*, and more. He currently lives with his partner and collaborator, artist PJ Adams, and their children in Baltimore, MD.

www.MichaelAnthonyAdamsJr.com

www.ingramcontent.com/pod-product-compliance
Lightning Source LLC
Chambersburg PA
CBHW031657040426
42453CB00006B/336